NERVE CONTROL

THE CURE OF NERVOUSNESS AND STAGE-FRIGHT

BY

H. ERNEST HUNT

DAVID McKAY
604–608 SOUTH WASHINGTON SQUARE
PHILADELPHIA

CONTENTS

NERVE CONTROL

CHAPTER I

NERVE CONTROL

THE subject of nerve control is of such first-rate importance to every artist and performer that it is indeed surprising that hitherto no attempts have been made to deal with the question in any scientific fashion or otherwise than by rule of thumb. However, since this is the case, it can be no matter for wonder that so many people, whose work necessitates public appearance or performance in some form or other, suffer under the disabilities of "nerves," and as a consequence fail to achieve all the success they deserve. Only too often do they find that the appeal which the value of their work should make, is neutralized by reason of this handicap of inadequate nerve control under which they suffer.

On the concert platform, in the pulpit, on the stage, in the public meeting, time after time we come across individuals who are capable of much more than they actually achieve, but whose every effort is weighed down by the hampering effect of nerves. The singer or the performer might have made twice the effect had he but been free from this burden of fear: the orator whose periods came haltingly and whose memory failed might otherwise have carried his audience with him in his discourse: the actor perhaps lacked the requisite poise and self-confidence to enable him to "get across the footlights": or the proposer of the amendment possibly made perfectly sound argument seem fatuous and unconvincing by the ineffectiveness of its presentation: thus in a thousand ways, as anyone may call to mind, this lack of nerve control, showing itself in countless forms, works to the undoing of the individual, and in frequent cases entirely closes the avenue of success against him.

Habit and use, which deaden us to the

acceptance of many an ill capable of remedy, have in this matter brought about a state of affairs in which nerves are tolerated as almost a necessary evil. Especially does it seem to be the usual thing for artists to be nervous, and many performers of the first rank are not ashamed even to confess to being in some degree at the mercy of their temperament. They always are nervous, or always have been, or they are nervous by nature, and so on, the reason varying in each case: but underlying all is the fundamental idea that the state of affairs is so, and therefore must continue to be so.

Now the whole object of this little book is to put forward the very opposite view, and to proclaim that the varied symptoms of nerves point straight to the lack of proper control: and that just as money is good in itself but bad money is likely to land its owner in difficulties, so nerves are an integral and important part of the physical structure, but bad nerves, disordered or uncontrolled nerves, are a source of discomfiture in any walk of life.

The English national type of character

is distinctly conservative and tends to make us tolerant of things as they are, to modify them only upon compulsion, and in general to trust to luck to muddle through somehow. It is not part of our inbred equipment to seek out the causes of things and find if it be really necessary for us to endure the ills we know. Rather, we are prone to acknowledge their existence and to get accustomed to them, and finally to accept them as the fit and proper accompaniments of our daily round.

Nature herself possesses a wonderful power of adaptation in the human body, and in cases of accident or disease will manifest features of compensation that are truly marvellous: such as, for instance, when the hearing of a blind man becomes super-sensitive to make up for his lack of the faculty of sight, or when one organ of the body takes up a function foreign to itself which is otherwise not being carried out in an adequate manner. But while the forces and workings of Nature may be said to be blind, though possessing marvellous powers of adaptation, we have on the other hand all the resources of intellect at our command, to question, argue and devise, and of will, to carry through and bring into being that which the brain may plan. It by no means therefore follows that because things are, they need always remain so: it is our first task to find out why they have become as they are. Very frequently we shall see that the state of affairs is due to perfectly ascertainable causes, though these were not at first apparent: then it will be observed that these causes themselves are capable of profound modification. Thus our investigation from facts back to causes will often show at once that we can so modify those causes, by the exertion of will, as to produce another and different set of facts entirely.

This then is the process which we shall follow in dealing with nerves. We will not, like the Christian Scientists, start by denying the existence of disordered nerves and the consequent evils (though it is better to do that than to submit tamely to their harmful jurisdiction), but we will investigate, and finally we shall discover that it is totally unnecessary for us to be at the mercy of our whims and fears. We shall find that temperament is largely a matter of growth, and that it is just as possible to construct an attitude of confidence, serenity and equanimity as it is to demonstrate that we are allowing these disorders and vagaries of our nerves to reduce our value as an effective force in life nearly to zero.

Many people know in a general sort of way that these and kindred ills grow alarmingly when indulged, and can only be overcome by the exercise of the will, which as a broad statement is perfectly correct. But when they are confronted with a definite case in which the nervous dread of some forthcoming performance brings on sickness or perhaps diarrhœa beforehand, and results in complete prostration afterwards, they are at a loss to see how any amount of determination can affect these physical ills. Especially so when the people who suffer thus are obviously the very last to have sufficient will-power at command to achieve what seems to them the impossible. Or if a person rises to speak upon some subject in which he is fully versed, and his memory suddenly deserts him, or if the vocalist is unable to control his voice so as to sing the songs he has so carefully studied, or if the pianist's fingers refuse to perform their allotted task,—is it sufficient to say to the unhappy individual that he is deficient in will-power and determination and that he should MAKE himself do these things?

As a matter of fact it would very frequently be quite untrue to say that he was weak-willed. Many folk of strong determination have nervous likes and dislikes that master them: multitudes of ordinarily strong-willed women lose their control at the sight of a mouse, some men cannot cure their nervous fear of cats, while numbers of otherwise rational people dread the dark. These overmastering emotions which are by no means infrequent cannot be adequately explained upon this theory of weakness of will; it does not fit all the facts. But through all these cases there runs the common factor which indicates their origin: the individual is at the mercy of his own nerves and controlled by them, and this in itself is abnormal and the very reverse of what ought to be.

Normal and properly balanced individuals have their nerves under control and dictate to them what effect they will be allowed to have upon the body: and yet in this sense it may be said that comparatively few of us are well balanced. Our fears, emotions and moods, as well as our likes and dislikes, are permitted to gain the mastery over us. We abrogate the command which it is so vitally necessary for us to hold continually over our forces, and then when the emergency or duty brings the occasion, and complete self-control is demanded of us, too late we find that we do not possess it. The will has frittered away its paramount authority in concession after concession, each one increasing the domination of the nerves and decreasing the supremacy of the individual himself. The stronger the will, the greater its power for construction as well as for destruction, just as a well-tilled garden if allowed to run to waste will produce a more luxuriant crop of weeds than the poor-soiled patch.

If then a person already has insufficient self-control, as evidenced by his present condition, it can do little good to tell him that he is weak-willed and must exercise more determination: the only rational way of helping him is to show the why and wherefore of his present state, by pointing out the perfectly natural method of growth which manifests its fruition in these nervous symptoms. Having thus, as it were, brought him back to the starting place, it is necessary to present a method of acquiring control by the development of will-power, in which direction and rule are substituted for concession and weakness, and by which ultimately a very high degree of control is manifested over the feelings and emotions. In this way the mentality is first brought under the dominance of the will, and then, since the mental and physical interact so closely together, it will be found that the bodily processes and the health come more and more immediately under control.

This then is the plan which will be followed in the succeeding pages. It will be shown that Suggestion is the basis of habit, both good and bad, but whereas haphazard suggestion may produce such detrimental results as are only too often experienced by those sufferers for whom this book is written, yet it is possible, by harnessing this mighty force, to turn its activities into useful channels, and by concentrating its energies in the desired direction to produce effects that in individual cases will seem little less than miraculous. In general, an absolutely confident and fearless attitude can be built up which will reflect itself not only in a complete absence of nervousness in public appearance, but which will also to a large extent illuminate the general outlook, strengthen and deepen the character, and bring a wholesome influence for good upon the general health.

CHAPTER II

SUGGESTION

SINCE the method for the cultivation of nerve control here advocated is one based upon the influence of suggestion, a few explanatory remarks are necessary. Suggestion is one of the most potent forces in the world, and yet it is one of the least understood by people in general, partly no doubt because its workings are entirely in the region of mind, and therefore unseen. But this very fact of being unseen and unrealized gives it an increased power, for it is a force that can be potent both for good and ill, and whereas an open enemy can be met and overcome, an enemy whose very presence is unsuspected lies in wait with all the chances of war in his favour.

Hypnotism and Suggestion have proved to be the discoveries which enable us to probe deep into the recesses of mind and to lay bare the processes below the surface:

and for the sake of putting the matter as clearly as possible we may proceed to illustrate our preliminary remarks with an experiment.

We ask the co-operation of a friend who is willing to assist: we bid him inter-clasp the fingers of his two hands, then to grip the hands tightly together and to imagine that they are so securely fastened that he is unable to separate them. In his mind we strengthen the idea by assuring him that when we have counted up to three he will indeed find his hands so closely fastened together that he cannot separate them, and that the harder he tries to pull them apart the tighter they will be fastened. We count up to three, and the seeming miracle happens: our friend tries to separate his hands and finds that he cannot. He feels as if all muscular action were inhibited and as if great weights were compelling his hands to remain fixed. Presently we tell him to stop trying, and then assure him that he CAN open the hand-clasp, or we may allow the idea to weaken of itself: in either case he is again able to resume the normal use of his hands.

Now from this simple experiment, which almost anyone can perform with a willing subject, we may deduce a whole range of facts of far-reaching importance. The illustration is, of course, of a most elementary nature but it embodies a most important principle.

It is obvious that in asserting to a normal individual that he cannot unclasp his hands we are putting forward an idea that is contrary to his expectation, past experience and common sense: of himself he knows that if he wishes to unclasp his fastened hands he can immediately do so. Herein lies the necessity of the reservation that he should be a subject willing to co-operate in the experiment, for if he be unwilling, or unable, to forsake for the moment the dictates of experience and to turn his mind actively on to a new idea, the experiment must fail: it follows from this that a strong-willed person accustomed to the directing of his own powers will prove the best type of subject.

It will probably be no less a surprise to the subject than to the operator when he feels himself deprived of all muscular action

2

in his hands and wrists: when he feels that his hands are indeed so pressed together that he is unable to unfasten them: and when his utmost physical efforts fail to undo the mental knot he has tied. The effect, it will be observed, lies in a different realm to the cause: the former is purely mental, the latter physical. On a second occasion the experiment will be more readily successful, and increasingly so until at length the effect can be induced practically instantaneously.

How is it that by means of a mere verbal assertion we are able to achieve a result that flies in the face of reason and all past experience? The answer lies in the dual character of mind: and the explanation of this one little experiment leads us also to the explanation of many of the seeming miracles of Christian Science and of other examples of psycho-therapeutics, as also of many induced diseases. In this latter classification we may perhaps include the subject under present consideration.

Mind is dual in character: there is that part of mind which lies above the level of consciousness, of which therefore we are

fully cognizant, and there is that part
which subsists below that level and of
which we are consequently unaware. Within
our conscious minds we receive the sense-
impressions of sight and hearing, smell,
taste, touch, and so on, and with it we
reason, argue, compare and remember:
but within that part which lies below the
level of consciousness—which we term the
subconscious—reside faculties of different
scope. Bodily processes, wonderfully intri-
cate in character and diverse in operation,
are carried on by the subconscious, and it
is a matter of common knowledge that
many of our everyday acts of routine are
carried out by the same means without our
active conscious control. What is it that
awakens us at a mentally pre-determined
hour in the morning? Where does that
word lie which is upon the tip of the tongue
which we are yet unable to recall by any
effort of will? It is not lost, for presently
when we are not thinking about it, back it
comes. Whence arises that sudden message
reminding us of some forgotten appoint-
ment or promise? Whence springs that
idea which we hail as an inspiration on the

spur of the moment? All these are but indications, slight in themselves but strong in their cumulative effect, of that great wealth of mind below the surface which exceeds both in scope and manifold activity the normal or conscious mind.

But wonderful as the powers of the subconscious are, there is one direction in which they are distinctly limited, and that is in the process of reasoning. It is capable of reasoning only in one way—deductively. If, for instance, a hypnotized person is told that he is swimming in water, he will deduce that he is wet, that he will need drying, that he must continue swimming in order to keep afloat, and other considerations of a like nature. But the subconscious is not capable of inductive reasoning, that is, of arguing from facts up to principles. As a consequence it is completely dependent upon the conscious mind for directive control, and in the position of servant devotes itself to carrying out or acting upon the commands or states which are suggested to it. In this connection a suggestion may be considered as an idea that is capable of producing an effect upon the mind, and the degree of ability of the mind to respond to and act upon ideas thus supplied is known as its suggestibility.

Here then is the explanation of our little preliminary experiment: the subject was influenced in the first case by the knowledge that he always had been able to clasp or unclasp his hands at will, but he was willing to let go of that belief and actively co-operate in impressing his subconscious mind, temporarily and in a very concentrated manner, with the opposite idea, that of impotence. The subconscious, unable to combat or argue as to the inherent unreason of the command, accepted it and acted upon it, and forthwith the action of the muscles was inhibited and the suggestion achieved its purpose. Under similar circumstances any other idea might have been put forward and as readily accepted and acted upon.

This is an example of suggestion in a rudimentary experimental form: but in actual practice we live all our days in a sea of suggestions which we are constantly accepting or rejecting according to our temperament. The suggestive effect of fashion is worth noticing: it may be that we regard some new fashion as a hideous innovation, presently we begin to get used to it, and finally we follow it: we have succumbed to suggestion. The social game of follow-my-leader, the political one of the same name, the religious belief which in many cases is not more than a subtly suggested and absorbed idea, the educational curriculum leading up to the university type of suggested but hardly individual development—all these are present-day instances of the wide sweep of suggestion.

It is extremely difficult to escape or get free from this influence which surrounds us from the cradle to the grave, but it is quite impossible for us to do so until at least we realize to what an extent even our most cherished convictions and habits of thought are suggested by our environment and up-bringing, our literature and conversations. However until we arrive at some degree of independence and freedom we shall continue to suffer from ills that need have no place in our lives, and to agree to and accept limitations and hindrances which have only such power over ourselves as we have given to them. It is because of this subtle suggestion that we accept nervousness with its thousand ills as natural: we see other people suffer and we are apt to think that we must suffer too, and, thinking so, it is perfectly natural that we should and do so suffer. But it is totally unnecessary.

Each experience that we undergo acts itself as a suggestion, and therefore each unlucky or unhappy appearance which is made in public adds to the suggestive weight until perhaps such an enormous mass of hopelessly bad suggestion is accumulated that it is little wonder that we begin to dread publicity. We fare worse and worse until at last our nerve is gone, and we become either neurasthenic wrecks or wholly incompetent performers, with the added sting that we know our capabilities are such as to make their mark if unhampered by considerations of nerves.

It will be necessary then, when we have fully considered the detrimental effect of undirected suggestion upon nerve trouble, to make the effort to gain some measure of freedom from adverse suggestion, **and** to develop a certain mental poise which will render ideas of any detrimental sort innocuous. The impression that because nerves ARE therefore they MUST BE is to be entirely abandoned, and with it all negative and enervating emotions. Things must be looked at in a more scientific light, facts must no longer be accepted at their face value, but their credentials and authority must be strictly investigated and, if need be, decried. When the clean sheet has been provided, then suggestion must be harnessed and set to do its directive work upon the plastic, absorbent sub-conscious mind. This in turn will react upon the physical organism and liberate it from a thousand hampering difficulties, setting it free to do its best work undeterred by any doubts or fears: strengthened with a new courage, a more active outlook, and with a broadened view of its own purpose and promise: and equipped with a know-ledge of the means whereby these **may be** assured of their due fulfilment.

CHAPTER III

SUGGESTION AS THE CAUSE OF NERVOUSNESS

IT will now be in place, since we have briefly shown the nature of suggestive effect, to explain what an important part suggestion plays in the production of unhappy nerve conditions, preliminary to showing also how the cure of these abnormal states is to be effected by the identical machinery which produced them.

Health is the normal state, and disease is a disturbance of that state. Health implies a proper co-ordination and development of the body and mind, for the interaction of both is so complete that any disturbance of the one is liable to upset the functions of the other. A lowered bodily vitality is answered by mental depression and weariness, by a pessimistic outlook and a whole set of deranged conditions varying with the individual. On the other hand, an

attitude of mental depression devitalizes
the body, diminishes the various glandular
secretions, depresses the circulation and
thus induces anything from a mere tired
feeling to that definitely lowered resisting
power to disease which is the direct invita-
tion to contagion and infection. In any
given case it may require skilled diagnosis
to ascertain whether the cause be mental
or physical, but we are nevertheless compelled by common observation to admit
this close relationship between mental and
bodily conditions.

Nervousness of the particular type with
which we are dealing may arise in the first instance either from the mental or the physical
side: it may also however develop from
suggestion, under the guise of conscious or
unconscious imitation, which may lead us
to suffer from those ills which we have seen
and known other performers undergo. But
if we take the cases in their order of fre-
quency we must first deal with those which
spring from a mental cause. Everyone
has to have a first appearance some time
or other, public performance is a thing one
can never take up in the middle, and

probably the first appearance is to the individual in its effect upon his mind the most important of all his appearances: here it is that he gains that great initial impulse towards thinking well of himself or ill, towards success or its opposite. We know that a successful first appearance gives a self-confidence which can hardly be acquired in any other way, while a failure at the commencement proves such a tremendous handicap that it is only the strong-willed or the doggedly persistent who overcome it.

The crucial point and the cause of all the difficulty lie in the fact that we are doing something for the first time, or under new conditions, and we have no previous experience or precedent to guide us and tell us how we shall succeed. Moreover, we go to face the ordeal, whatever it may be, as regards nerves, in a more or less unprepared fashion. We wonder, we doubt, we fear, and our mental expectation hovers between hope and mistrust. This then is the critical moment, and once we surmount it in safety we are more optimistic as to our future, and once we fail we have added immensely to our coming troubles.

The larger—subconscious—mind, to which we previously referred, has one marked characteristic which bears directly upon this point: it possesses a memory which is absolutely non-forgetting. This memory holds the record of every thought and impulse, every act and experience which has come within our ken. They are each of them graven indelibly upon the tablets of our mind, they form our record, our character and our most real self. That this is so, a little thought will soon give indication, if not proof: for delirium, intoxication or sleep can quickly bring memories to the surface which have long been normally forgotten. Hypnotism enables the subject to recall many things to mind from the buried past: insanity, which is often due to an abnormal subconscious usurpation, may do the same. Across the drowning man's eyes is said to flash the vision of his whole past life, not merely the episodes he seems to remember: and old folk, whose normal memories are hopelessly failing them, frequently have the most vivid recollections in their second childhood of the remote events of seven, eight or more decades ago.

These mental impressions are not merely as dead records in pigeon-holes, forgotten and futile, they are on the contrary actual living influences below the surface of mind, and according as the record is harmful or helpful so are the promptings and tendencies which arise therefrom for the future occasion.   If fear thoughts have in the past been constantly entertained and as constantly recorded it cannot but happen that all the future likelihood points to fear, that fear promptings will inevitably arise when the occasion offers.   It would be no less than a miracle were a courageous disposition to be reaped from such a sorry sowing. From fear thoughts comes fear, from courageous thoughts courage: no other is possible, for every thought is nascent action.

It is now possible to discern the reason for treating fear impressions and failure thoughts as of such great importance: they can NEVER be forgotten, they are henceforth part of the thinker's mental equipment.   He may dismiss them, he may think he has forgotten them; they are out of sight but not out of mind.   They are items he himself has inscribed upon the debit side of his mental balance sheet and he must pay his debts in full. Failure itself intensifies the fear idea many times, and with each fear thought the cumulative record grows and its suggestive effect becomes greater and more insistent. It must be remembered that at any given moment the action or state of mind is determined by the dominant or ruling idea in the mind: consequently by anticipating failure (or doubting success, which is much the same thing), failure is rendered certainly the more probable and complete success by so much the more difficult of attainment. The process is not irrational, indeed the only wholly irrational thing would be to expect anything else: and when once the twin ideas of an absolutely unforgetting memory in the subconscious, and a mind immensely susceptible to suggestion are grasped, then the wonderfully strong effect of the mental attitude upon the body with regard to nervousness can at once be seen.

Trouble having a physical origin is frequently seen when a temporarily lowered state of vitality results in impoverished nerves, and consequently some nervous instability or distress. The lack of nerve control may be solely due to this temporary depletion of the physical forces, but it has to be remembered that each symptom produces and records its own mental effect. Each failure is permanently registered in the mind, and acts as a suggestion predisposing to further failure: and it not infrequently happens that when the state of health improves and the actual cause of the nervous difficulty is removed yet the difficulty itself remains, owing to the acquired mental habit which acts as a permanent suggestion. The cause has now been transferred to the mental realm, and no amount of tonics, sea breezes or pills will make the slightest effect, except in the most roundabout of ways through the influence of the general health. Many cases of stammering are directly traceable to such a cause as this, and the only efficacious remedy is a re-education of the will by some form of suggestion. Any habit or attitude of mind tends to persist unless counteracted by some opposing tendency or suggestion, and each repetition engraves the idea more deeply upon the brain, whether it be fear, nervousness, ill-health or anything else, and most emphatically the body will react in consonance with the mental impression.

It will now be tolerably plain that the process of inducing nervous troubles is a matter of the steady and persistent accumulation of fear and failure ideas, which in course of time produce an overwhelmingly strong effect upon the mind, and thence upon the body. The will-power of the individual, so far as this one point is concerned, is reduced to a negligible quantity. He is powerless in the grip of this fear-phantom in his own mind, to which he himself has given birth, dominion and power. If he desires further confirmation of this, let him look round at his friends and neighbours and see how they too are in the grip of fears and doubts of no less power, which they are firmly convinced they can never conquer or remove, and by that conviction do actually render null and void any efforts they may persuade themselves to make in that direction. Fears of old age or for a rainy day, fears of bad health, bad trade or bad luck, fears of new experiences and of meeting new people— these are the phantoms which dominate and limit to an utterly absurd degree the minds and powers of ordinary individuals: and by no means the least of these fears is this dread associated with public performance, with platform work, with coming "out of the ruck," which renders a few plain words upon the subject so very necessary to-day.

The imitative nervousness referred to above is simply another variation of the workings of this same suggestion. To an impressionable nature it is quite sufficient to have seen or known an artist or a speaker suffer from nervousness or some other disability. The idea lodges in the mind and cannot be forgotten, it recurs and is again recorded at intervals: each repetition is again recorded, until finally the one original .idea grows into a lusty crop of similar ideas, which later manifest in action and thus proceed to bring forth their progeny at a still more alarming rate. The process is quite usual and commonplace but none the less exceedingly serious, for, unless counteracted, it culminates in the individual losing (as so many do) all mental elasticity and vigour, and becoming instead a mere mass of rigid ideas, likes and dislikes, stereotyped opinions and hard-and-fast routine. This is a state of premature mental degeneration and is followed by its bodily consonance, stiffness, rigidity, premature old age and probably some form of disease.

But if the process which induces these mental and bodily ills in countless thousands is plain, it is surely no less plain that it is far from inevitable, and that it only exists in proportion as we concur from ignorance or inertia in its being so. To demonstrate the avenues leading to freedom from these undesirable conditions will be the purpose of succeeding chapters.

CHAPTER IV

SUGGESTION AS THE CURE OF
NERVOUSNESS

HAVING briefly outlined the nature of
suggestion and the part it plays in the
inducement of nerve troubles we must now
turn to the constructive side of the question,
and we will proceed to indicate how this
great unseen force can be brought into
use as a help to freedom and liberation from
these hampering difficulties: for while it
is most assuredly necessary to recognize
its destructive effects, yet its constructive
possibilities are of far greater importance.

The very simplicity of the method and
its freedom from all cost and parapher-
nalia may, paradoxically enough, perhaps
militate against its acceptance on the part
of a few, since human nature is apt to
rate the value of things according to what
they cost. How consistently fresh air and
pure water are undervalued: and so too

is the equally free power of thought. But
the money standard is entirely useless as
applied to the subject of suggestion, and
the sole test of such a method of nerve
control as this is that of actual trial.
Academic argument as to its possibility,
its likelihood, its permanence or anything
else is beside the mark: the only test is
that of experience, and this will demonstrate anew, as has been amply demonstrated before, that the intelligent user
of auto-suggestion will liberate himself
from a hundred ills, and will be able to
build up a temperament upon lines which
he himself may determine.

The two fundamental facts upon which
the whole process of upbuilding is based
are those pertaining to the subconscious,
which are both vital and capable of demonstration, viz. that the subconscious memory
or record is perfect, and that suggestions
planted therein are accepted and acted
upon, irrespective of their present truth.
This latter characteristic gives us the extraordinary power of definitely fixing upon a
given type of thought or habit (in which
perhaps we may be conspicuously lacking)

and, by the use of will, gradually but absolutely incorporating it in the temperament. The effect of suggestion can be achieved in two ways: the first is by the use of a particularly strong suggestion impressed once or twice with much vigour, or when the natural suggestibility is heightened, as in the case of the hypnotic sleep; and the second is when the suggestion is not so vigorously impressed, but the effect is gained by the constant reiteration of the same idea. This latter process is the surer of the two, though the slower: but it is particularly applicable to self-treatment or auto-suggestion, and therefore at the service of everyone, irrespective of circumstances, time or place.

There is a certain bias in the lay mind against hypnosis which is quite unreasonable and unjustifiable when the treatment is in trustworthy hands. But such bias undoubtedly exists, and we can only hope for a more enlightened state of public opinion to remove it. There are dangers, of course, arising out of the unscrupulous use of hypnotism, but they are immensely exaggerated: and in every case the ultimate responsibility rests with the individual who agrees (as every subject must first agree) to be hypnotized by a charlatan, without even taking the commonsense precaution of having a third person present to act as a check upon the suggestions given. However, in the case of auto-suggestion this question does not arise, for no one is concerned in the matter at all except the individual himself. Moreover, there is no sleep state, and the whole process may be regarded in the light of a rational and scientific exercise in the training of the will. Obviously also the value of the exercise is greatly increased by the consideration that, with the development of the will, the purposes to which such increased control can be applied are by no means confined to nerves, but can be directed to other points specially applicable to each particular case.

We now proceed to take a typical illustration of a nervous state in order to show exactly how to set to work to combat the difficulty. Let us suppose that our subject is shortly to give some public performance, and the following are extracts from actual

letters received portraying the general run
of symptoms which we may expect to meet.
A says, "Although I have played in public
for years, I can never do myself justice on
account of my nervousness. About a year
ago I had a nervous breakdown and since
then I have lost nearly all my self-confidence." B puts her case thus, "I have
performed in public on the piano and organ,
and have to do so in about a fortnight's
time. I suffer terribly from nervousness
before the time, and from exhaustion afterwards." While C remarks, "If your method
cures me I shall be everlastingly grateful,
as mine is one of the worst cases I have
ever heard of. I can neither sleep nor keep
food down if I have anything to do in
public."

It will at once be noted that in each case
we have the nervous dread to eliminate,
which we will do by inbuilding the idea of
perfect self-confidence in its stead: in one
of the cases we have also the symptoms of
sleeplessness to combat, together with the
inability to retain food, and in another we
have to deal with the point of subsequent

exhaustion. The only thing we absolutely must stipulate for as a condition of success is work, honest and whole-hearted work, a few minutes every day without exception: and that indeed is a small price to pay for so great a deliverance. It is also presumed that our subject is familiar with these earlier chapters showing the connection between past thought and present nerve distress.

The next step is to draw up a set of suggestions, about four in number, which will deal with the nervous dread by implanting in its stead the idea of self-confidence, and we formulate the following:—

1. I AM ABSOLUTELY SELF-CONFIDENT.
2. ON THE PLATFORM I AM PERFECTLY COMFORTABLE AND AT EASE.
3. MY NERVES ARE ABSOLUTELY STEADY, NOTHING CAN DISTURB ME.
4. I AM FIT AND STRONG AND GIVE OUT THE BEST THAT IS IN ME.

These should be written out on a slip of paper and then memorized. They have now to be built into the mind: and at first five minutes at a time will be ample for the exercise. This should be done in the morning, during the day, and again a night: occasion should be chosen when there will be no interruption, and in a place where quiet can be obtained. The subject must then be seated, and with the slip of paper before him the written suggestions must be firmly and forcibly impressed upon the mind, one by one. The virtue, of course, does not lie in the actual word but in the state of mind which the words depict, so that the exact frame of mind postulated must be very vividly imagined and brought into being. Mere idle repetition of a formula is worse than useless. The idea has first to be created in thought, and then forcibly and repeatedly impressed upon the subconscious mind, and the desired effect will then in time fructify into actuality according to the suggestion. This exercise should be continued daily for a week, and then the suggestions should be changed for another set dealing with additional points, such as:

1. MY NATURAL ATTITUDE IS CONFIDENT AND COURAGEOUS.
2. I ENJOY AND LOOK FORWARD TO PUBLIC PERFORMANCE.
3. I AM STRONG, AND FEAR IS UNABLE TO ENTER MY MIND.
4. ON THE PLATFORM I AM QUITE AT EASE, AND DO MYSELF JUSTICE.

These must be inbuilt in the same way as the others, and then after an interval changed again. As a variant to silent thinking let the suggestions be decisively whispered, and again be forcibly spoken aloud, since thus they reach the brain through another avenue of sense.

As regards the suggestions themselves there are one or two points to be noted: for instance, all the ideas to be inbuilt are positive, there are none which say "I am NOT . . ." this, that, or the other. When we set to work to overcome a negative condition we do not oppose it, for very frequently the direct opposition arouses a kind of instinctive obstinacy which merely serves to increase the original difficulty. Instead we circumvent it, and by inbuilding its opposite very strongly and definitely we "overcome evil with good." It is obvious that there can only be one dominant idea in the brain at a given time, and in an emergency that idea will be automatically predominant which has the largest and most powerful backing in the subconscious. If fear has been the emotion that we have most frequently entertained and registered in the record of our past thinking, then the idea of fear is henceforth to be denied admittance into the mind, so that it will be unable to fructify and grow stronger. At the same time courage is to be suggested and given existence in thought, consistently and persistently, until as a mere mechanical question the volume of recorded courage-thought outweighs that of fear. Once this is achieved the bias and natural promptings turn towards courage and bravery, and the impulse to fear is so far overcome. This is turning to very practical use the knowledge of the unforgetting and indelible record of thought in the subconscious.

Another point to be noticed with regard to the suggestions is that they are comparatively short and concise, while the object of putting them in definite form into writing is to ensure that the idea is reiterated in precisely the same form again and again. The same effect would not be produced by suggestions which differed in detail from day to day, even though they might be of somewhat similar type; it is necessary to get the concentrated effect of this reiteration. A diffused attack is comparatively harmless, but a concentrated attack is many more times as effective: the wise advertiser knows this point from observation if not from science, and he consequently chooses either an enormous and striking advertisement once, or else he makes his appeal by smaller suggestions reiterated in the same form until they are recognized and assimilated (though probably quite un- or sub-consciously) by the possible customer.

Our suggestions then must be inbuilt, and the more frequently the better: and since by concentrated effort the effect of a purposeful suggestion is many times stronger than that of a casual impulse, it follows that though a habit of fear, for instance, may have been many years in the acquirement, yet its overcoming can and should be much speedier by reason of the more intense application of the will. While the process is not and cannot be instantaneous, yet the progress is both sure and certain, and the visible improvement manifest in a comparatively short time gives the worker further confidence and encouragement to continue.

CHAPTER V

SUGGESTION AS THE CURE OF NERVOUSNESS (*contd.*)

THE suggestions we have hitherto utilized, it will be noted, have not definitely opposed the nervous fright of performance, but by aiming at creating instead a positive attitude of comfort, ease and confidence that effect will be achieved and the fright eliminated. A thing cannot be both black and white at the same time, though it is quite conceivable that it may pass through grey stages in its transition from black to white: so also there will be transition stages in the change from nervousness to confidence. In like manner we shall avoid directing our suggestions to the contradiction of the symptoms of sleeplessness or sickness, and we aim rather at supplanting them by more desirable conditions. If we actually ARE sleepless that in itself acts as a suggestion, and frequently a tolerably

42

strong one, especially if the insomnia is of some long standing. If then we assert "I AM SLEEPY," much energy has to be expended in overcoming the suggestion already there to the effect that insomnia is actually making its presence felt, and after a balance of forces is produced there is but little energy left for efficacious positive suggestion.

It is far better to circumvent the difficulty and assert as a general suggestion, "I am strong and well," and then during the day time, when there is no question of sleeping or being able to sleep, to inbuild such an idea as "At night I sleep soundly and naturally." Here we touch upon a phenomenon which partakes of the nature of what is known as "post-hypnotic suggestion." If a person under the influence of hypnosis be told that at some future time named he will experience a certain effect or do a certain thing, he will at that time feel that effect or do that particular thing even though the hypnosis be long terminated and his condition perfectly normal. He feels an irresistible influence at work, though he may be totally unable

to account for it.   Therefore in thus
arranging during the day time to sleep
soundly at night the subconscious is given
what practically amounts to a post-
hypnotic suggestion which takes effect at
the stipulated time.

The idea which many people possess that
when one is suffering from acute insomnia
it is only necessary to affirm "I am sleepy"
is thus shown to be fallacious.   The acute
insomnia is itself such a strong suggestion
that no ordinary process of affirmation is
likely to overcome it, except in the case of
individuals who have strongly developed
their will-power.   In the same way when
one suffers from acute nerves on the platform the mental affirmation "I am not
nervous," employed as a species of forlorn
hope, is rarely efficacious, because of the
opposing suggestions of actual fear.   These
are remedies which are being handicapped
out of utility by the wrong manner and
time of their application.   The "spade-
work" of suggestion must be accomplished
in silence and quiet where there is no
opposition or interruption to mar its effi-
cacy: yet as the control grows with prac-

tice, ultimately a very forcible command might, if the will were well developed, restore the lost mental control even in an acute case. But for the average person it is necessary that the work should be done when and where conditions are favourable.

The exhaustion following upon public performance can be overcome by the use of a similar method, suggestion being directed toward conserving the nerve force and to obtaining comfort after the ordeal. It will however be found that as the poor and ineffective nerve control constituted the primary basis of all these ills, so the gradual strengthening and restoration of that control will automatically lead to an improvement in these symptoms, however varied they may be in character, even without any direct suggestion. The direct method can be used for the alleviation or cure of any particular difficulty, or when speed is of more importance than slow and steady growth: but in a general way the upbuilding of a positive control will surely lead to the extinction of most of the unhappy results which have arisen from a lack of it. Different individuals suffer in varying ways from the vagaries of nerves, and some of the troubles seem at first sight to have but little connection with their source, but whatever they are there need be no dismay. Each of them must be due to a cause, and in the vast majority of cases that cause will be found to be ill-regulated suggestion, and the remedy therefore is obvious.

Some symptoms may be of very long standing and consequently deep rooted in the mind, and it may prove necessary to apply local measures as well as general suggestion, and to take that particular symptom, whatever it may be, and re-educate the mind with regard to it. Suppose, for instance, that a pianist's fingers WILL persist in feeling stiff during performance in spite of the use of suggestion, one might start work by building day after day a series of ideas leading up to the desired suppleness, somewhat after these lines, "MY FINGERS ARE SUPPLE AND LOOSE." Strongly affirm this, and then in the mind's eye picture the fingers as desired. Carry the idea into practice by extending and stretching the fingers in exercise several times, making a point of feeling this suppleness and looseness. Then affirm, "MY FINGERS HAVE COMPLETE FLEXIBILITY, THEY ARE LOOSE." Stretch them again and feel the depicted looseness: then "THEY WILL ALWAYS BE SUPPLE, ALWAYS." This however is only a type method of working which can be extended and addressed to the remedy of any undesirable trait, with results which will prove surprising to those who are unaware of the extremely close and vital connection between mind and body.

We know that a mental emotion can produce very strongly-marked physical effects, as may be noted in the case of blushing. There a passing emotion, a fleeting thought, in an instant suffuses the face and neck with colour. Fear also, by inhibiting the supply of blood, blanches the cheek, or at another time may cause a profuse perspiration over the body, thus demonstrating the very close and intimate connection between the mental and bodily processes. It will thus be evident that by learning to control the mental side of our nature and determining the emotions which are to find lodgment in our minds, we can to a large extent dictate our own physical conditions. Occasionally we find a pianist whose hands under the stress of nervousness become so moist as to make the keys slippery: or we may come across a vocalist whose throat becomes excessively dry, or who must needs swallow at the critical moment in his song: or we may meet the instrumentalist whose fingers refuse to warm up: all these and similar cases will in time prove amenable to this mental treatment, while many of them will yield almost at once.

The system is not put forward as a miracle worker, but the limits of its application are as yet only dimly apprehended: in practical use it will work against all sorts of handicaps which would seem to offer it but scanty chance, for while the direct consequences of lack of nerve control are fairly obvious, the indirect consequences ramify in such bewildering fashion that the inexperienced may well be pardoned if they fail to connect cause and effect. The elasticity of suggestion is by no means its least valuable asset, for it can be used to combat any undesirable trait. Concentration in this mental work is especially necessary, but if it is found that there is difficulty therein, then such concentration must as a preliminary be developed and inbuilt: if regularity and perseverance be stumbling blocks, let them be implanted in the form of suggestions. Even if there be a lack of interest, let that interest be supplied by the same means, for since any desired quality may be incorporated in the mind, we have the unique privilege of building according to our own chosen pattern. Nor is faith essential as a starting-point: it matters not whether we believe suggestion is going to prove successful or not, let us but do the work and do it thoroughly and well, and then the issue will show indubitably enough that the theory was sound. The results, of course, may be more striking with faith than without, but whether there be faith or not, the subconscious must and inevitably does remember, and the mind consciously or unconsciously does absorb the reiterated suggestions. With faith the seed is planted and nurtured under the best conditions:

lacking it, the seed is thrown down to take
its chance, and most frequently it will
come up, but the growth is always a struggle
against odds.   The catch-phrase or the
catch-picture of an advertisement often
remains with us though we have paid no
conscious heed to it: and every teacher
is familiar with the way in which children
"absorb" knowledge, and how in course
of time that knowledge sticks, in spite of
all lack of interest and application on the
part of the pupil.   In like manner reiterated suggestion achieves its object, even in
the face of an unbelief.

Our subject who suffered from intense
nervousness, sickness and exhaustion has
now been working for perhaps a fortnight,
three five-minute periods each day, and
the improvement is already noticeable.
The nerves are steadier and more under
control, there is a greater feeling of "grip"
over the whole body, the insomnia is
departing and the sickness and exhaustion
are gradually ceasing.   In six weeks the
condition will be very markedly improved,
and in as many months a self-confidence
will have been built up such as nothing can

disturb. Public performance will have then become a pleasure, the vitality and health will be much strengthened, and with this will come a very distinct increase in that undefinable power known as "personality." All the forces of the body will be co-ordinated into one purposeful unity, instead of warring one with the other, and this means that an harmonious self will take the place of one weakened and distressed by internal discord.

Such may be expected to be the course of the average case: after six months the process will have achieved the purposes immediately in view, but it will also have opened a window upon a new vista of self-development which the wise will be very unwilling again to close. Will-power as applied to nerves is invaluable, but applied to health it is priceless: and it may obviously be applied to temperament and technique, to memory, to fluency of speech or finger, or to any one of a hundred uses. Take the case of a person who with a lack of flexibility is trying to play or sing some florid passage. Stop for a moment and discuss the question: point out the hamper-

ing effect of stiffness and then ask him to
relax his rigidity, and then bid him "think"
the passage through quietly and with the
desired flexibility several times. Let him
then repeat in action what he has conceived
in his brain. The resulting freedom and
elasticity will prove an object-lesson in
"mind over matter." The experiment
can be tried in the same way in connection
with drawing or dancing, or with any
physical movements in which flexibility
is aimed at and rigidity hampers. Success
must in some measure depend upon the
ability of the teacher adequately to depict
the desired conditions, but in any case the
difference before and after should be most
marked.

We are thus encouraged to cultivate will-
power, so that by our minds we may
dominate and dictate our own physical
conditions in lieu of being dominated by
them: and this method of auto-suggestion
is the crux of the cure. But there are many
general considerations and side issues which
have a bearing upon the subject, and some
of these will be dealt with in succeeding
chapters. However, the main lines already

laid down are applicable to all, in whatever particular branch of performance or platform work they may be engaged, and each should formulate the special suggestions which may be applicable and **advantageous** to his special case.

CHAPTER VI

CREATIVE THOUGHT

IT will now be evident that in our efforts towards eradicating nervousness we are undertaking no less than a reconstruction of the whole mental attitude. Whereas in the past our view of things has been coloured by the haphazard experiences of everyday life, without any definite scheme of formative influence behind it, we are now starting on an educative process with certain very concise and predetermined aims, which we are inbuilding daily for short periods with concentrated effort. But unless we get a clear impression of the work we are doing and the principles we utilize, it may perhaps appear that by our attitude during the rest of the day we may neutralize the good we obtain from our spells of concentration. It cannot be too clearly understood that there is no magic in the suggestion formulæ, and that the

54

mere reiteration of the words so many times a day is of itself likely to prove of little value. The underlying importance of the words is in the picture or idea that they convey: we think in mental pictures, and of these the written or spoken words are but the visible or audible symbols. The words must therefore be turned into ideas and as such be impressed upon the mind, the state depicted must be imagined and visualized as vividly as possible and the idea kept constant in the mind during the time of concentration.

But side by side with this it is also necessary to let go of all ideas which conflict with the thoughts we inbuild. It would be futile to expect a few minutes' concentration daily on courage to outweigh the rest of the day spent in nervous dreads and anticipations: there would, indeed, be magic in the formula that could accomplish this. Auto-suggestion is not going to take the place of effort, it is not going to enable us to sit at our ease and have success come to us for the asking, anything we get at no individual cost does us comparatively little good: but it is, on the contrary, certain to call into action the latent powers we possess, and it puts into our hands the key to the marshalling, directing and utilizing of these great innate forces.

It is vitally important, then, that during our daily avocations we should endeavour to live up to the suggestions we inbuild, and not neutralize them by saying one thing and acting another. If we are suggesting fearlessness then at all times we must try to be fearless and to carry ourselves as if we were indeed so. What is likely to be the effect of a self-suggested fearlessness combined with a cowed and dejected bearing? Obviously the two things do not tally, and one or the other must perforce tend to become untrue, and the one which is least perpetuated in action will gradually be overcome by the other. If we start to inbuild fearlessness let us keep it always before us, be it, live it, and act it, and in these circumstances it is simply unthinkable that the fear can continue for any length of time. As a matter of fact it cannot and will not continue, we shall grow, insensibly perhaps, into the new suggested pattern and it will become our normal type of mind.

There is the very greatest importance in a mental attitude, in our outlook upon things, for it is a trite but none the less true saying that we each of us view things differently. A word, a phrase, an object or a circumstance may appeal to several people in as many different ways, inevitably coloured by the mental bias of the individual. A person filled with fear looks upon public performance in an entirely different fashion to the man who has self-confidence and fears nothing: yet the circumstances are the same in each case, it is only the mental outlook that compels the one to regard it as an ordeal to be dreaded, and the other to consider it as an opportunity to be welcomed. Hence the importance of so attuning the mind as to turn public performance into the latter blessing rather than the former woe. When at length this sanity of outlook is completely built up, then things and events have only that effect upon our minds that we allow them to have.

Suppose we have the fact of an actual

past failure to reckon with, some breakdown or non-success upon one particular
occasion: everything, absolutely everything, then depends upon how we regard it.
If we keep the failure thought present in
our mind and accept the idea of having
failed, then is confusion worse confounded
and we shall experience the greater difficulty in freeing ourselves and rising again:
but if the attitude is one tuned to bravery
and success, the failure makes no deep
impression, but rather stimulates to further
exertion.   History is full of instances
where men have struggled through failure
and impediment to ultimate success solely
by dogged and untiring persistence, by
the mental attitude which first pictured
and then demanded and achieved success.
The true scientific basis for this lies in
auto-suggestion: these men have won
through because instinct has led them to
develop their will as the power by which
they achieve, but suggestion places the
same possibilities at the direction of each
one of us, only in a more decisive and concentrated way, and since it has a scientific
knowledge underlying it, with a surer
prospect of success.

We are thus led to the point when we see that success firmly and continuously built into the mind results at length in success in a material way, just as surely as failure thought predisposes to and attracts actual failure: in other words, the thought becomes habit, which in turn solidifies into character, and this ultimately manifests itself in circumstance. It may seem at first a far cry from mere thought to its crowning result of failure or success, but the chain is there, and the sooner we realize that the determining factor in a life is this power of thought, then the sooner we can set to work to obtain control over this force of forces. Recognizing the harmony, the extraordinary consonance between the mental and the bodily states and material surroundings, will bring home to us, perhaps more than anything else, the utter and vital necessity of refusing any longer to allow our thoughts and impressions to accumulate at haphazard.

A nervous, unstable temperament frequently manifests itself in irritability, hysteria and possibly dyspepsia, with a corresponding instability in the financial and domestic affairs. A timid, frightened and dejected temperament similarly involves itself in anæmia or morbid despondency, with a certain depression and lack of circulation in pecuniary matters. A fearless and optimistic temperament consorts with free circulation and robust health and with comfortable surroundings. These consonances follow more or less upon the basis of temperament: suppose the fearless and optimistic man were to turn timid and pessimistic, it is tolerably certain that his prospects would change and his health deteriorate. It is not far-fetched therefore to sketch this chain of cause and effect as an additional argument for the development of thought control.

In point of fact, modern research is bringing home to us more and more this wonderful correspondence between the thought and the material worlds, and is thus taking away the last shreds of responsibility that we have been so apt to place upon chance, luck or circumstance, and is putting it ever more directly upon our own shoulders: in a manner too which we can in nowise escape. While this may indeed give some of us pause, at the same time it opens up a prospect of achievement before each and every one of us which should be most exhilarating, since we now have the weapons in our hands with which to hew success. The proper study for mankind is man, and it will prove most valuable for each reader to try and trace in other people's lives, as well as in his own, this consonance between the mental states and the health and circumstances. He will then learn in time to understand that folk are where they are exactly because their outlook, temperament and abilities have fitted them to be there: and because for that reason they could not be anywhere else. Had their characteristics been different, they would of necessity been elsewhere, for if a person is in a position for which his abilities do not fit him, the resulting friction is simply nature's effort at readjustment, and it will continue until he at length finds himself in circumstances for which his characteristics are suitable. On this reasoning it follows that the responsibility for health and circumstances, as a broad general truth liable to modification in special cases, rests ultimately upon the individual himself, and the motive power for any improvement lies in thought, and the primary point of application is in the development of the will.

Little by little this will become more evident to the thoughtful inquirer, and the searchlight must then be turned inwards, and whatever is wrong or undesirable in outer circumstance must be traced inward to its source. As a personal question this is both more difficult and less gratifying than in the case of other people, but it is nevertheless a very necessary process. Since, however, we are working specifically at nerve control it will be well to deal with that point first, and to defer the consideration of development in other directions until success has been obtained in this primary matter. All the time the will is being trained and strengthened, and such development can be turned later in any desired direction, and every success achieved will in its turn act as a suggestion guaranteeing the success of the method and offering a valuable return for the trouble and time expended.

The necessity of active co-operation with the spirit of the suggestions is now obvious, and they must be backed up by careful attention during the ordinary round of everyday life. This co-operation involves, as before mentioned, the definite dismissal of all thoughts and ideas conflicting with the general tenour of the suggestions, and again it must be emphasized that refusing to entertain an idea by a blank negation is false policy. Do not attempt to meet force by force, but overcome evil with good: turn the thought into some other and more useful channel, or supplant it with another and better thought. Do not try to dam the river and so cause a great flood which must sooner or later break through, but divert its course into a direction where it can do service. Merely to say, "I will NOT think this" is to cause it to come up with redoubled persistence: think of something else. It will soon become habitual to let detrimental thoughts slide and to entertain only helpful ideas, and then continual co-operation with the sense of the suggestions will become easy, and

will enhance their effect instead of
neutralizing it.   Moreover, the results of
the suggestions are cumulative, for the
subconscious mind retains every impression
and absorbs it, so that whether or no the
effect be at once apparent, each thought
has played its part and has fulfilled its
purpose and is acting as a foundation for
other thoughts of like nature.   The sowing
of the seed is the thing that matters, the
harvest follows by unalterable law.

CHAPTER VII

PLATFORM WORK. SINGERS AND PERFORMERS

WHEN we come to deal with public performance, and especially with musical work, we learn that suggestion may be applied in various ways which are not evident at first sight, and one of these is in the defining of the spirit in which the artist approaches his task. In the last chapter the point of "like attracting like" was mentioned, but the theme will bear development. There exists a close parallel in thought to the phenomenon of sympathetic vibration in sound. Everyone is aware that if two tuning-forks vibrate to exactly the same note, and one be sounded, that the other will vibrate in sympathy: the vital essential being that the consonance or attunement between the two should be perfect. Thought and emotions are vibratory in essence, just as sound, light and

65

heat; and different emotions have different shape waves and varying wave lengths distinctive to themselves. Each of these emotions tends to arouse a sympathetic emotion in minds receptive or capable of response: we are all aware of the contagion of fear, the infection of laughter, the sympathetic bond of a common sorrow, the unity of a common aim, and so forth, and all these are illustrations of the working of this law of sympathy.

This same law works just as surely in the case of the performer as in any other, and perhaps more so, for an audience by its position as audience is always ready to listen, receptive and prepared to be influenced (especially so, it may be mentioned, if they have paid for admission), while the artist fills the part of suggester, operator, or transmitter: much therefore must depend upon the impression an artist consciously or unconsciously radiates. If he takes the platform with nervousness as his predominant emotion he suggests his own discomfort and distress in the minds of his audience, and this emotion reinforced a thousand times surges back upon him to his own undoing. In practical experience most of us know this at first hand, and probably from both sides of the footlights: the obvious remedy is to have some elevating or helpful idea so strongly impressed that it has become the normal attitude of mind. It may be the idea of pleasure or sympathy, goodwill or welcome, of dominance or interest, but it at any rate should be one of the positive and stimulating emotions, and it will assuredly be of the greatest assistance in obtaining a larger measure of success. Not to think about the matter at all and merely to step upon the platform as a person rather than as a personality is the royal road to mediocrity.

In addition to having the mind attuned to a feeling of ease and confidence, care must be taken that the carriage and attitude upon the platform further bear out this idea, for the whole mien inevitably acts as a suggestion of power and ability, or otherwise, upon the audience. If the mental attitude and the outward bearing support one another, so much the better, but it is mere waste of time to allow them to be mutually antagonistic.

No one can be favourably impressed by a timid, shrinking, or semi-apologetic manner on the part of a performer, nor by a person who is unable or refuses to meet his audience eye to eye. We are naturally enough assessed at our own valuation until or unless we in other ways disprove it, hence the necessity of thinking "grit" into ourselves and living up to it. Mannerisms too are a pit for the unwary, as well as an occasional source of advertisement to the unscrupulous: the singer who has some petty trick, such as raising his eyebrows for a top note or clearing his throat before beginning to sing, will find that it is his eyebrows or his cough that attract the attention of his audience and for which they wait, much to the detriment of their appreciation of his music. Any little point such as this can at once be cured by a few well-directed suggestions, so that there is no excuse for the pianist tossing back his unruly hair as a habit, unless indeed he finds that it adds to the fascination of his personality.

Singers and instrumentalists alike will find it much to their advantage to dispense with the actual copies of music altogether during performance, the whole attention is then so much more free, while the singer can at once make his appeal to the audience by means of his eyes. So soon as the visual connection is made, eye to eye, the thoughts, emotions and impressions seem to pass along the beam like the electric impulse along a wire. To dispense with music, of course, requires the cultivation of memory, but here again if suggestion be used and the idea be implanted that the memory is strong and that a song once memorized cannot be forgotten, together with other suggestions of a like nature, no insuperable difficulty will be experienced in this connection.

Much may be done in the way of memorizing work by silent practice away from the keyboard or without voice. Simply do all the brainwork required, and hear or see in the imagination the work being performed as it should be: this will have quite a marked effect, and it enables vocal practice to be carried on during a heavy cold, and instrumental practice where no instrument is available. In this way also freedom of voice and flexibility of finger can be much facilitated: this imagining or visualization method can be applied to very many things in the daily life, as well as to the general bearing on the platform and to the details of performance: with practice they become impressed as habits upon the subconscious mind, and then during the actual performance, when not infrequently the subconscious usurps control, these are the channels in which the thoughts naturally run and to which the actions conform. This temporary usurping of control by the subconscious accounts for the unusual renderings given on the spur of the moment, for the almost spontaneous variations of time and expression, and for those little flashes of inspiration which go towards a characteristic rendering when the performer loses himself in the music. The phenomenon is akin to inspiration, and yet in its surrender of conscious control first cousin to madness and therefore hardly to be recommended: but the work at silent mental practice will tend to limit these flights on the part of the subconscious, or at least to confine them within the bounds prescribed by conscious control.

The diction can be greatly influenced by this method, for when once it has passed the mechanical stage it becomes a subconscious process, all the various movements being co-ordinated, registered and expressed through the nerve centre of speech. As the subconscious is directly amenable to suggestion we have here the most concise and efficacious means of correcting and eliminating faults of diction in lieu of the slower and more roundabout way of influencing the brain by reiterated muscular practice of the desired result.

The interpreting artist should ever keep in mind his special purpose, which is first to apprehend the spirit of the musical message, and then reinforcing it with his own vitality to give it forth to his listeners. To this end he has to fill the rather difficult position of an intermediary, in sympathy both with his audience and the spirit of the music, and the measure of his sympathy is the measure of his ultimate success. This ability to give life and vigour to the musical thought or emotion is not so much a question of technique as of personality: those personalities which impress us we recognize as of the positive type, those which fail to score we designate as negative. This is the question of temperament, which is apparently so obscure in its origin that it is generally considered to be a gift of the high gods and impossible of development: a view which is quite wrong. It cannot be denied, of course, that some people possess it in marked degree and others not at all, yet it is entirely unnecessary to suppose that because we do not happen to enjoy this great gift of a positive temperament we must for ever go without it. In point of fact, apart from broad and general modifying influences such as health, sex and age, it is principally dependent upon the type of thought that has been habitually entertained, and of which as a consequence the character has been built.

Gentle thoughts long entertained make a gentle temperament, one that is softening and persuasive in its influence: energetic thoughts build up a character to correspond: the mind habitually used to command seems to radiate authority: so that broadly speaking we determine our personality and the effect it produces by the type of thought we entertain. We know that it is possible to inbuild very strongly any type of suggestion we choose, whether we have that characteristic already within us or not, and therefore it must be possible for us to develop a personality tending towards any desired type.

Naturally, in dealing with this question, the individual will exercise a wise discretion as to what he attempts to inbuild, so that he does not produce any "misfits," for though all things are possible yet not all things are desirable. All, however, should endeavour to incorporate in themselves a wide and understanding sympathy and such an element of the divine discontent as shall drive them to seek ever higher aspiration and attainment. Then, again, just as in the early stages we insisted upon the proviso that the spirit of the suggestions in actual use must be adhered to during the rest of the day, so we have to realize that personality which is such a vital platform asset is as great an asset in the everyday life off the platform, and its spirit must ever be remembered.

It is idle to expect to be a sympathetic interpreter of love themes upon the platform before the public and as hard as nails in private life: if the sympathy is to ring true it must be both deep and sincere. It is possible, of course, to simulate this sympathy and to deceive the unthinking multitude for a time, but it is absolutely certain that the most deluded person of all is the individual who thinks to achieve in this way anything more than the fleeting success of an hour.

Suggestion is an immense power, and when it is thoroughly or even partially understood, it is capable of application in a thousand ways that go deep down to the foundations of our being: but its perception also lays upon us a great responsibility. If we truly realize what it can do, we have but little excuse for setting our standards low: the limits to our achievements we ourselves set, and the influence that we wield, be it in song or from string or keyboard, is determined solely by the depth of the thoughts that vibrate in our inner selves. Nor does the effect of our efforts remain with ourselves, but it radiates out in every direction and affects for good or ill every one of those whose hearts are attuned and capable of responding to the message that our own heart sends out.

CHAPTER VIII

PLATFORM WORK.   SPEAKERS AND PREACHERS

IN dealing with platform work with special reference to speakers, much that has already been said with regard to singers and performers will be found applicable, for the general principles underlying each are identical.   The question of personality is perhaps more important to the speaker and the actor than to the musician, and the value of good delivery cannot be overestimated.   The speaker, moreover, has, as a general rule, the entire burden of occupying the attention and holding the interest of his audience, which is not always so in the case of the musician.

We will now turn to some of the points which specially concern the speaker, whether in the pulpit or on the platform, and we assume that he comes to face his audience with an attitude of some positive nature, as mentioned in the previous chapter. He rises to speak, and at once the questions obtrude themselves, is he to speak from manuscript or notes? Is the discourse to be prepared word for word, or is it to be extemporaneous as to its manner of expression? Or again, is it to be completely extempore? Each of these methods has its exponents, and it remains for us to discuss which is the most generally useful and the one likely to be most widely applicable.

We must rule out of account for general purposes the discourse or address to be read from manuscript: such should be reserved for those cases in which an absolute and recorded exactitude of expression is necessary, for the read word rarely carries with it that same weight and interest with which the spoken word is invested. As a rule, the reason for reading the discourse is not one of advantage, but of distrust on the part of the individual in his ability to carry through the speaking successfully. This distrust can be promptly eradicated and supplanted by confidence, and the validity of that reason then disappears.

6

The discourse may, as a matter of preparation, be written first and afterwards delivered from memory, but even so it will probably seem to the listener to lack spontaneity and life.

Reading also fixes the eyes upon the manuscript and breaks that eye to eye connection which has already been referred to as most valuable. It restricts the use of gesture and facial expression, and in ordinary cases these disadvantages far outweigh anything that can be urged in favour of the read discourse. In less degree, much that has been said of the manuscript-delivered speech applies to that which has been prepared word for word, the utterance is trammelled and the imagination fettered, while a chance interruption may throw the whole thing out of gear. The purely extemporaneous address is not to be recommended save under the spur of necessity; the tongue is an unruly member and has been known ere this to run away with its owner, leading him to say things on the spur of the moment that on reflection he may have cause to regret. Moreover, the faculty of "thinking on one's legs" is one that as a rule requires a considerable amount of practice.

The method which will be found best in the majority of cases is that of the discourse mentally prepared beforehand and arranged under sequential group headings, which may or may not take the form of written notes: at first notes may, and probably should, be used, but the speaker ought to aim at complete independence of external aids. The qualifications necessary for this can each of them be inbuilt by the use of suggestion: the first requisites are confidence, assurance, and calmness, and to these in early chapters we devoted much consideration: another point is the memory, which again responds very quickly to suggestive treatment. Fluency of diction is also a fundamental, and can be acquired by direct suggestions such as—

"I AM NEVER AT A LOSS FOR A WORD OR A PHRASE."
"MY THOUGHTS FLOW EASILY AND I EXPRESS THEM FLUENTLY."

In this way any existing difficulties can be

overcome, and all the conditions that are necessary for fluent speech can be gradually and effectively built into the mind.

At first sight it may appear that this asserting the idea of fluency is a very superficial way of inducing it, but the reverse is really the case. It must be remembered that it is upon the subconscious mind that we are laying all these commands, and it will respond, for it possesses latent powers and capabilities undreamed of by the average man: by means of suggestion we learn to harness some of these innate forces which until we begin to direct them are more or less blind. In support of this assertion one or two points of common knowledge may be cited by way of illustration.

An insane person, in many cases, is one whose conscious control is abrogated, perhaps only in one or two particular points, and who is dominated by his subconscious: the actual physical strength of a maniac is proverbial. Consciousness serves to limit the application of one's total powers, so that if, for instance, a normal person can lift, say, 150 lbs., in a subconscious state he might very well lift 300 lbs. A fit of blind rage, which is a state parallel to temporary madness, gives this same access of supernormal strength. The somnambulist, in a subconscious condition as he is, achieves feats and runs risks and dangers and triumphs over difficulties which he could never even face in his normal condition. Abstruse mathematical problems are occasionally worked out by subconscious processes while the mathematician sleeps, poetry is written and stories are produced while their authors play no conscious part in the doing. In fact, we know that in certain directions the subconscious powers greatly exceed the conscious, even to the extreme manifestations of thought-transference, clairvoyance and telepathy.

Knowing this, then, it will be less difficult to credit the assertion that, by putting the subconscious to perform that which we normally cannot do, we may achieve what would almost seem to be the impossible. But the student of the mind very soon learns to be chary of that arrogant word "impossible," and as he investigates some of the vast powers laid at his command by understanding, he sees that "impossible" is merely the dogma of ignorance. The possibilities of interworking between the conscious and the subconscious minds are among the most vivid and valuable of modern discoveries. Spasmodic and haphazard intercommunication explains many of the seemingly unaccountable things of which we hear from time to time: the second sight, the warnings, the prophetic dream, the death vision, spontaneous thought-transference and similar occurrences. But it is difficult to see what limits can be placed upon the beneficial and constructive effects that may result from an organized and controlled interworking. Genius is the result of the subconscious faculties working hand in hand with conscious control: when, combined with the conscious as expressed in reason, argument, comparison and logic, there are intuition, foresight and unfailing memory.

There need be no scruple in demanding from the subconscious results of which we are ordinarily incapable, and for the hesitating speaker to demand fluency is, on this line of argument, by no means such an extraordinary thing as at first appears.

If our hesitating speaker were to be hypnotized, and in that state were to be told that he could give an eloquent and fluent speech upon a given subject and were ordered to do so, he would do it without difficulty. All that we are proposing is that the speaker should derive the same effect from continued auto-suggestion, and it CAN be done, but the doing is in no way likely to be assisted by a preliminary fixed idea that it is impossible. In this sense faith is a condition of success, for the very obvious reason that active dis-belief (that is, active belief to the contrary) is a counterbalancing suggestion which must at any rate weaken those we are using. The open mind, combined with the willingness to accept after proof fresh ideas and new lines of thought, is all that is requisite to secure the best effects.

After a little work at these suggestions it will be found that having once resulted in the desired condition they become habitual and automatically reinforce themselves. Consequently they must be taken in order, commencing at the most necessary and fundamental, and, as each step is mastered, there is the surer foundation for building the next, until at length the seeming miracle may well have been accomplished. The hardest work naturally comes at the beginning, which is also the period of the least apparent result: but this will disturb no one who realizes that at first the chief work of the suggestions must be to neutralize the old suggestions that have grown up as chance dictated. It is only when the old habits of thought are finally balanced that actual constructive work really commences.

Lastly, let the speaker, failing a natural and effective style of his own, adopt a good model for his work and one that is adapted to his own innate qualifications. On broad principles a fast delivery should be avoided, since it presupposes a mental agility on the part of his audience which they may not possess: speech is very rarely too slow. Vowel sounds are vocal and carry, consonants do not: it is therefore essential that consonants should be exaggerated in order to allow for the inevitable "loss in transit," in order that they may reach the audience in their proper proportion to vowel sounds, thus making intelligible words instead of incomprehensible sounds. Much value may be made of pauses which give the listeners time to assimilate the argument: a breathless speaker in his haste causes his hearers to suffer from acute mental fatigue, and thus he defeats his own object. It is also well to observe in speaking the relative rests which are indicated in the written scheme by punctuation marks. The usual devices of inflection, emphasis, varied pitch, rhetorical questions and so forth will doubtless be employed as avoiding any tendency towards monotony, and all these can be worked out by mental practice, while with each discourse they become more and more part of the speaker's mental equipment.

But the most important point of all is "what to say," for all our consideration so far has been devoted to the question of "how to say it," and this is essentially a matter of the mental and intellectual grasp of the individual. Yet even here our new-found powers by no means desert us, for we have but to turn this mental machinery to higher things and it will assuredly be no less helpful than when dealing with what may seem to be mere matter-of-fact exigencies. But here we begin to approach subjects that transcend the immediate scope of these remarks, and for the moment we must resume the consideration of facts which concern our main theme of nerve control.

CHAPTER IX

HEALTH

No one who endeavours to obtain any real degree of nerve control can afford to neglect or minimize the importance of health. A lowering of the general vitality from any reason whatsoever must necessarily show itself at once in diminished nerve control, the precise form it may take varying of course in individual cases. But the whole nervous system is quick to show the results of any decrease or impairment of the normal blood supply: very frequently the voice will give indication of some loss of nervous energy long before it manifests itself in the grosser physical ways. The care of the health, then, is a matter of distinct weight to the person who aims at any degree of balance.

The cardinal points which pertain to the physical side of health are reasonably obvious: adequate lung development, sufficiency of food and drink, perfect elimination of the waste products of the body, sleep, and economy of effort. Now without a doubt the point where modern civilization fails in its fitness is in this matter of elimination. Here is the ultimate cause of at least nine-tenths of the physical ills that beset us in various forms. We live, of course, in a highly artificial state of civilization and the natural functions have been compelled to adapt themselves to wholly unnatural conditions: in addition to this comparatively few people have sufficient knowledge of physiology to be aware of what really is the normal working of the body. False modesty also steps in and declares that some perfectly natural processes are things not to be talked about, and the result of such ignorance as necessarily follows is not infrequently grievous and disastrous.

The working of the bowels is one of the most vital of the natural functions, since it concerns the elimination of waste and poisonous matter from the body. Food passes into the stomach, already in the first stages of digestion from the action of the saliva in the mouth: there it is further acted upon by the various digestive juices and ferments, and it passes thence into the smaller intestine where the assimilative processes are still further carried on. From there it proceeds into the larger intestine, and finally the waste residue is expelled from the body. There is no valid reason why one should eat four meals a day and allow the waste matter to accumulate, for in this accumulation lies the danger: bacteria multiply, and poisons are bred which, being absorbed into the blood, carry their baneful effects into every part of the body.

Headaches, neuralgias, indigestion, sore throat, lassitude and depression are among the most common and direct results of this auto-poisoning from neglect, while many more serious complaints, infectious and otherwise, are indirectly due to the lowered state of vitality thus induced. Appendicitis, for example, is always known to be preceded by a history of constipation: no words can be too strong in insisting upon a regular and frequent elimination, or in condemning as unnatural, unhealthy, and unclean the attitude of those who content themselves with an elimination every two or three days, or even every week.

This working of the bowels is largely a matter under nervous control, and is therefore particularly susceptible to suggestion: pills, purges and medicines of any kind are thoroughly to be deprecated, and it is at least questionable whether the ills the remedies produce are not worse than those they are supposed to cure. Suggestion will always in time secure regularity, though its efforts may have to be backed up by physical exercise and attention to diet. On no account, save in exceptional cases, should salts or other aperients be resorted to, since any natural function supplanted by artificial methods tends to become weakened and finally useless. White bread is a prolific source of constipation, as also is much meat: substitute brown whole meal bread, more vegetables and fruit, with cheese and nuts as an occasional alternative for meat, and any difficulty will then largely solve itself.

As regards sleep, each must be a law

unto himself, no hard and fast rules can be laid down: but a sufficiency is imperative, and warning should always be taken by any hesitation or confusion in speech of an unwonted nature, for these and similar symptoms are often the advance-guard of threatened trouble. A proper supply of breath is also essential for the body: with less than a certain amount the body cannot live, with an insufficient or vitiated supply it can only exist, and an ample supply is a necessary condition of vigorous health. It is not here proposed to detail a series of exercises for the development of the lungs, this pertains more directly to physical culture, and there are many excellent little manuals devoted to the subject which will amply repay the perusal and practice. It is quite possible for the body to accommodate itself to a deficient supply of fresh air, but this process is not to be regarded as in the least analogous to health, which is indeed far more than the state of being "not ill." A sparrow put under a bell glass may die of asphyxiation in ten minutes, but if another sparrow be introduced into the vitiated atmosphere at the end of three minutes it will probably be dead at the end of another three, not having undergone the process of "getting used to it" as the first sparrow did. The mere fact that the body can "get used to" living on a depleted supply of oxygen offers no valid reason for regarding it as other than an unhealthy process.

Suggestion can be combined with the physical exercises to produce excellent results: it tends to fix the mind upon the action and its expected results and thus favours their fulfilment. These suggestions may run somewhat as follows:—

1. THIS EXERCISE STRENGTHENS AND DEVELOPS MY LUNGS.
2. I FEEL MY VITALITY AND VIGOUR INCREASING EVERY DAY.
3. THE BLOOD COURSES IN MY VEINS INVIGORATING ALL MY BODY.

Further types of suggestion should now be unnecessary, for the reader will have apprehended the principles upon which to work and will be able to construct his own: but let it ever be remembered that these are commands laid upon the subconscious, which achieve their effect in part owing to the intensity with which they are given, and in part owing to the cumulative effect of the reiterated suggestion. The present truth or falsity of our affirmation matters not at all: it is a future condition that we postulate.

It is well to note the effect of casual suggestion upon the body so as to be on guard against any ill-health arising from a mental cause. Complaints which occur periodically, such as weekly headaches, should be looked upon with some suspicion, for wherever the element of regularity enters it is more than probable that unconscious suggestion or expectation is playing a distinct part in causing the difficulty, and conscious work in such a case can as certainly cure it. The mere idea that certain articles of diet are indigestible is often taken by the subconscious as a suggestion, and indigestion after partaking of them is the natural result: both the cause and the remedy are mental.

A draught of itself is innocuous, but a draught combined with the idea that it is going to give cold is nearly certainly harmful, mainly because the subconscious believes and makes it so. "The thing that I feared is come upon me" contains a lesson which is fully explained by the workings of the larger mind: whatever we fear in our minds we thereby tend to attract in our circumstances, and that same fear inhibits our resisting powers and renders us an easy prey to its effects. Fear is a potent cause of ill-health, as also are all of the negative emotions: fear, anger, jealousy and rage are all of them typically bad emotions and engender definite toxins or poisons in the body which produce their depressing or harmful after-effects. The person who suffers from habitual ill-temper suffers also from auto-poisoning and cannot expect to be either healthy or well. The worrier depletes his powers and vitiates his own efforts and scatters his all-important health: he cannot in reason expect to be robust and strong.

In all these forms of ill-health we again find the mental factor as the originating cause, and we therefore know the remedy which has to be applied in order to remove the outward manifestation. Interaction between the mind and the body is so close that we cannot improve or lower one without making a corresponding alteration in the other, and so as we gradually tone up the mind the health follows suit, and thus makes possible further mental progress.

It may seem that suggestion has to be applied in so many ways as to be bewildering, and perhaps it might be so if everything had to be done at once, but in reality it is a gradual process, and the first thing to be done is to cure the obvious defects arising from omission or commission that present themselves to us. As progress is made step by step further progress becomes more rapid and easy: greater control is acquired and facility in auto-suggestion increases and the erstwhile difficulties drop off one by one. Then arises a danger in that self-satisfaction may consent to the dropping of regular work: the danger will by no means be self-evident, and it will be probably only after an experience of ill-luck or want of success, or a general feeling of "losing grip," that the individual will again be driven to the conclusion that it is at all times necessary to keep the bodily forces strictly and definitely controlled by the mind.

Health which gives of itself a feeling of optimism—that it is good to be alive to-day and that to-morrow is worth looking forward to—carries with it a certain vital influence which radiates from the body and can be felt by others. It is our duty, as well as our highest interest, to cultivate and develop this, for it grows and varies with our mental and physical states and has no little to do with that subtle power of personality to which we have before referred.

Here our strictly material considerations have taken us somewhat below the surface and space forbids that we should pursue the subject further, but for those who wish to do so there are other opportunities. Our concern is strictly to insist upon health as a prime condition of nerve control, and to indicate the lines upon which health should be sought, and to give warning of some of the pitfalls which yawn before the path of the uninstructed health-seeker. The claims of suggestion to regulate health are not far-fetched or exaggerated, though it is certain that they are yet ill-recognized and decried. But again, there is no standard by which we may unfailingly judge of a claim, save that of experience, and we can only urge that it is this one test—that of actual trial—which we are anxious to have applied to the system advocated in these pages.

CHAPTER X

TUNING UP

HAVING outlined the way in which auto-suggestion may be used not only to eradicate nervousness and to gain control of the nerves, but also to secure a degree of self-development attainable in no other manner, a few general remarks for those who essay to come before the public will not be out of place. It matters not in what precise character one has to come forward, whether as performer, executant, singer, speaker, preacher, lecturer or debater, there are certain broad considerations that apply in every case.

By the mere fact of public appearance it is evident that a positive or radiating position is taken up, as opposed to the negative or receptive: it is a case of giving out and transmitting. This presupposes that there must be something to transmit, and this is the first point that requires our notice. It will be generally admitted that the spoken word conveys a greater impression than the printed, that the song finely rendered creates a more marked effect than ever the printed copy can do, that the sermon delivered with personality behind it carries more weight than when issued in book form from the press: it is this underlying something, this additional factor, that makes an artist out of a mere performer, a genius of a clever man, and an orator out of a speaker.

The point is no new one, it has been dealt with at some length by no less a writer than St. Paul, and his conclusions stand absolutely and undeniably right to-day when he says, "Though I speak with the tongues of men and of angels and have not charity, I am become as sounding brass or a tinkling cymbal." The world abounds in tinkling cymbals, they tinkle on the concert platform, on the stage, and even in the pulpit, and often they must wonder why their tinkling produces such small effect: but rarely do they recognize that it is because they themselves are without charity—nothing. The object of this little

book has been primarily to demonstrate
the cure of nerves: but inasmuch as this
has necessitated explaining the method of
application of a force that, innate in all,
is yet undiscovered in most, and the setting
in motion of wide-stirring energies, it is felt
that without striking this deeper note of
increasing potentialities and greater re-
sponsibilities as the underlying motive of
all, this book itself might lie open to the
charge of being mere machinery without
a heart, and without charity—nothing.

Directly one gets below the surface of
things and forsakes the commonplace
ground of eating, drinking and making
merry, there are so many things intimately
interbound that claim our attention, one
leading on to the other, that it may well
happen that having opened the magic door
the quest may take us farther than ever we
thought to go, but whoever would learn
must travel, and whoever would travel
must learn. As soon as we deal with this
problem of nerves we learn about the
power of thought, we begin to see how
characteristics are brought into being, we
see character and personality in the making,

we discern the seeds of success and failure
that later bloom into fate and destiny, we
see a new philosophy of life in formation
and we shoulder a new responsibility.
We mark how the onus of praise and
blame is taken from the circumstances of
our birth, education and environment and
placed upon our own type of thought.

We begin to shake free from the shackles
in which we have unwittingly grown: we
realize that our fears, dreads and despond-
encies, and in many cases our actual ill-
health and our privations, are due to the
limitations we unconsciously absorbed in
our thoughts and attracted in our lives.
The one message which all these things
combine to chorus out is—"Realize your
freedom, your innate powers, your possibilities and your essential divinity." Until
they are realized in thought it is impossible
that they should be achieved, and it is
hardly likely that they can be realized in
thought while the whole organism admits
the symptoms of defeat all along the line
—nerves, ill-health, poverty and despair.
The whole situation can scarcely be better

summarized than has been done by James
Rhoades in the lines—

> Again that Voice, that on my listening ears
> Falls like star-music filtering through the spheres,
> "Know this, O man, sole root of sin in thee
> Is not to know thine own divinity."

If a tuning-fork vibrates to D, it is impossible that it should respond to the call
of a G fork, and if our whole attitude
vibrates to these lower tones of impotence
and failure then the call of our divinity and
high heritage may sound again and again
and we shall be unable to hear. We have
no spiritual ears to hear. We must set to
work to tune ourselves higher by the power
of thought and suggestion. We know that
no thought goes unrecorded, but that each
leaves its indelible mark in raising or
lowering the balance of thought, which is
the essence of character. We know that
under the influence of suggestion the subconscious will accept and act upon ideals
that we in our conscious selves are yet incapable of realizing, and therefore beyond
question we possess the power of tuning
ourselves upward in the direction of those
ideals. This it is to vibrate to the higher

tones of being and so to learn more of truth. This is the only learning that weighs anything in the truest scales, the learning of charity or, in its honester name, Love.

The singer may sing with every guise of art and every trick of technique and yet fail to make of his singing a thing of life: a tinkling cymbal, indeed, or as sounding brass! The preacher may have every oratorical device at his fingers' ends, he may "read well in print" and have a faultless delivery, and yet his personality may give the lie to his discourse. The instrumentalist may have every note, phrase and accent perfectly correct and still fail to give even the semblance of life to the music: none of these are able to infuse the dry bones with life—with love. So, we may cure nerves and ensure the completest comfort on the platform, but if the performer is to aim at no more than that, he will discover that the success he thought to attain still eludes him. He will have crossed one stream only to be confronted by another, and yet the power that took him across the first can also take him across the second and all other streams. With this free-given power of thought he can attune himself to whatever he wishes, and if he be wise he will daily concentrate his attention and inbuild such thoughts as will tend to raise his mental attitude to a higher plane and a yet higher still.

There are many books that will help to raise the ideals and instil ideas of hopefulness and power, a short list of which will be found in the appendix, and the perusal of any of these will lead to the discovery of other and kindred volumes. As the realization that the thought-world is the realm of cause, and the material world is the realm of result, dawns upon the reader, many of the olden landmarks may possibly come toppling down and new ones have to be erected in their stead, but the old ones will never fall until they are undermined by the advance of new truths. Moreover, new and all-powerful weapons are being placed in the armoury of him who has the courage to break free from convention and look at things as they are. Change is a condition of growth, and the divine discontent is the very antithesis of that

stagnation which leads to decay. Thought-
power and suggestion open up new worlds
of possibility, and while the number of
those to whom the subconscious and its
faculties are familiar is as yet infinitesi-
mally small, nevertheless present indications go to show that in the future this
will be one of the supreme and vital factors
in the development of mankind.

When an organ tuner is tuning a reed
pipe he has another note sounding in order
to give him the pitch, and he tunes up or
down the scale through all degrees of dis-
sonance until the pitch of his pipe nears
that of the sounding note. Nearer and
throbbing nearer it comes, waking a tensity
of expectation which continually increases
until finally it is merged into the satisfaction that arises from complete unison.
Much akin to this is the feeling of the artist:
there is no satisfaction to be obtained by
him or his audience without that sensation
of sympathy so essential as a bond between
the two: but the preliminary "tuning up"
cannot be done upon the platform, and if
the sympathies of the artist be insufficiently
elastic to run the whole gamut of the

emotions, it may prove impossible for him to reach just that particular note to which his audience can respond. This is another aspect of that most excellent gift of charity, for where love has widened the sympathies it will be found that they automatically tune up to the attitude of the audience: but self-interest, self-seeking, and self-importance vibrate as a very constricted and inelastic tone, the very reverse of sympathetic, and consequently it is extremely unlikely that any lasting or successful appeal can be made.

For a lack of success the fool will find a thousand excuses, yet the wise man will not look for excuses but for faults in himself, faults both of omission and commission, not only on the surface but below it; and when they are recognized they can be cured. No one who has his own progress at heart, whether as a business man or as an evolving spirit, will be unwilling to learn; but against the dead wall of self-satisfaction there is not much save time and distress will prevail. A hide-bound self-complacency no doubt shuts out a good deal of petty annoyance and ensures its owner a certain amount of animal comfort on his way through life, but it is a state of intellectual mortification and the very negation of progress.

Then lastly, but by no means least, we place among the qualifications necessary to achieve any success worth having, a willingness to learn. Cultivate an active sympathy that will respond to poor as well as to rich, to sorrow as well as joy, seeing the common bond of humanity betwixt all. Let charity be the mainspring of life so that the spirit underlying the spoken phrase or the melody of song be that of love, unselfish love. On the platform and off let this influence irradiate the life, giving poise and confidence to the bearing, and carrying with it an aura of vitality and health to which none can be indifferent. In the realm of thought overcome evil with good, and plant the garden of the mind so full with beautiful flowers that there is no room for noxious growth or disfiguring weeds. When this is accomplished there need be no anxiety as to the ultimate result, no question as to success, for as like attracts like so shall all the effort be crowned a hundredfold with its predetermined fruit.

CHAPTER XI

CONCLUSION

IF we briefly recapitulate what we have said upon this important subject of nerves it will be remembered that after emphasizing the undesirability of accepting nervousness in its thousand forms as a necessary evil, and proclaiming the freedom of the individual as a state attainable by all, we proceeded to discuss the cause of nerves. This we ascribed to suggestion, and we endeavoured to point out in the briefest fashion how suggestion works and what an intimate bearing the subconscious has upon all these mental problems.

The primary characteristics of the subconscious we stated as its amenability to suggestion and control by the will, and its unforgetting memory: these being the two main factors that contribute to the formation of character. Suggestion acts, we showed, as the pattern-maker for the

subconscious to build upon, while the unforgetting memory retains as a living com-
ponent force in the mind every impress
received. Thus it appeared that every
fear-thought, every nervous dread, every
frightened anticipation, and still more
every actual failure was a living force
working in the mind to the individual's
undoing: we pointed out that all too
rarely were strong and courageous thoughts
entertained in sufficient strength or number to outweigh this bias towards fear and
nervousness,· and since of necessity the
physical symptoms correspond to their
mental origins such was the cause and
development of nerves.

This being so it was no long step to the
idea that the inbuilding of thoughts of
courage, ease, confidence and comfort,
systematically and in a concentrated
fashion, would in process of time modify
and counterbalance the previous fear-
thoughts and entirely outweigh them in
the mind: which is but the step preliminary to supplanting actual nervousness with self-confidence. Whether the
ideas suggested and inbuilt were true or

8

not mattered not at all, for the subconscious does not argue about the truth or falsity of the ideas but simply acts according to their direction. Moreover, the cumulative effect, due to the fact that subconsciously nothing can be forgotten, was sure and certain.

Here therefore we say that given the two premises of these faculties of the subconscious mind (and though they are very far from being generally recognized, yet they are capable of demonstration), the argument for this method of cure is both reasonable and conclusive. As regards the results, provided the requisite work is intelligently and continuously done, there can be no doubt. Time and again we have watched cases where this control was gradually acquired and immense benefit derived, not only with respect to nerves but also in more general ways. Subsequent chapters were devoted to the particular consideration of matters that pertained to the musical performer and to the platform and pulpit speaker. The problem of health as it appeared in the light of suggestion was then presented, and finally a more intimate view of the questions opened up by the powers of auto-suggestion was put forward. It now only remains to add a few remarks of a general character in conclusion which may help to make more secure the effectiveness of the method advocated.

It has been already pointed out that fixed opinions are themselves in the nature of suggestions, and that therefore if the new suggestions are to operate in the most effective manner, the fixed opinions (where they clash) should be held in abeyance, so that some approach to an open mind may be the attitude with which this subject is approached. Faith is not strictly necessary, the absence of prejudice being sufficient: but a fixed idea that it is "all nonsense" will, of course, secure its own result and render progress impossible. Yet curiously enough it is precisely this same principle— that the idea strongly held and entertained secures its corresponding physical effect— upon which we build: the only difference being that we utilize the principle to ensure progress, and our disbelieving friend uses it (unconsciously) to deny and prevent any such result. His power of suggestion is a two-edged sword, and wielded intelligently it can conquer circumstance, but if unintelligently, it wreaks the harm upon the individual himself.

It is not to be anticipated that progress will be instantaneous; a word has been said upon this point before, but it will bear repetition: the process is a building one, and stone upon stone must be laid before the design of the edifice becomes apparent. It is, moreover, extremely difficult to indicate specific periods for a cure, since individuals vary so much in their initial starting-point, their will-power, concentration, intelligence and application, but it is not too much to say that even a fortnight's work will demonstrate that there is "something in it," and progress thereafter will become much more rapid. Should anyone fail to secure any effect, there will be found to exist fundamental defects in himself calling for remedy. It may be, for instance, that he is incapable of concentration, in which case all the energies and suggestions must be directed to the attainment of this one characteristic since it is fundamental to the others, and it is also the one that is most likely to beset the unsuccessful worker.

Continuity is a very necessary point to which attention must be paid; a path is made across a field by frequent walking in the same track, no effect is produced by an aimless wandering over the meadow once a week. Similarly "brain tracks" are made by the constant and consistent reiteration of the same idea. Occasionally misguided people write to say, "I am saying your suggestions over every day, but they do not seem to do me much good," and this shows that they have not even comprehended first principles. It is hard to express a criticism more succinctly than is done in the Bible, "Not every one that saith unto me, Lord, Lord, but he that DOETH. . . ." In precisely that way it is the man who merely "says" the suggestions over who finds them fail, and he that "doeth" achieves his end: exactly similar is the difference between "wishing" and "willing." Therefore in case of any lack of success first look for the failing in yourself, and after that it will probably prove unnecessary to decry the system.

Man is master of his fate. Too long have people been at the mercy of conventional ideas which have restricted their usefulness and ability: here and there outstanding men have set out with an ideal that they firmly intended to, and consequently did achieve, while lesser men wondered and ascribed it to luck or chance or favouritism. The lesser man follows the line of least resistance and admits that birth, education and circumstances are his masters, and consequently to himself he suggests impotence and powerlessness. The strong man refuses to admit limitations, sweeps obstacles aside and wins through by the sheer force of determined thought. By this same power the little man is armed with the identical weapon that the bigger man uses, and he can aim as straight and hit as hard: yet even so he must continue to fail so long as his only battle-song is, "I cannot, I cannot."

Man is the master of his fate, and every knock and every shrewd blow that he receives should serve to point out some weak spot, as is, indeed, the sole plan and pur-

pose of Nature's knocks and blows. Each
pang of nervousness, each mental dread is
a warning cry that there are weaknesses
calling for redress, each pain is a symptom
of internal trouble, and not until that
trouble is redressed and the weak spot
strengthened can the pain vanish and the
blows cease to fall. When confidence takes
the place of nervousness there comes no
more nervous ills, for their warnings are
no longer needed: having achieved their
object they vanish. The cause lay within
the mind, but the effect was manifested in
the body: always from within, outwards.
The things that are seen are temporal,
but the things that are not seen are eternal.
Thus is demonstrated the futility of thinking to cure things that have their root
within the recesses of the mind by attacking
the outward symptoms. So simple and
commonplace thing as a headache, what
is its rational cure? Is it a headache
powder? That merely removes the symptom of a greater ill, and temporarily, for
since the cause remains the effect will
surely re-occur again. What was the
cause of the headache? It may have been,

as it often is, impure blood. And what made the blood impure? In all probability insufficient elimination. What was the origin of this? Either ignorance or carelessness. These are mental causes in the ultimate, and that headache is in nowise really curable save by the enlightenment of that ignorance or the eradication of that carelessness. The headache is but the kindly warning drawing attention to that mental defect which, unless remedied, will lead, after yet more stringent and emphatic warnings, to some serious trouble.

Thus seeing the marvellous consonance between the mental and the physical, and the beneficent purpose of seeming ills, the understanding reader will have ready to his hand many of the materials necessary for the construction of a stimulating and workable philosophy of life, and he may be emboldened to going some of the way towards agreement with the statement that man IS master of his fate. By the time he has arrived at this conclusion he will probably be unwilling to forego the advantage of a short daily concentration: in the rush and stress of modern life it is

increasingly difficult to keep a valid hold
of the things that matter without some
such aid, and yet unless we are going to
keep that entirely necessary grip upon the
tiller of our ship of state we shall find that,
instead of sailing a straight course, we are
driven hither and thither at the mercy of
every gust of circumstance, with all its
inevitable loss of harmony and happiness.
Just the few moments' concentration every
day is the sovereign remedy for a thousand
ills, and it costs nothing, for all the vital
gifts are free and yet are beyond price.

So may the curing of this little ill of
nerves, which is but a single symptom of
a larger impotence, be but the opening of
the eyes to a greater and grander view of
life, and may the same power that achieves
its end in substituting confidence and
courage for nervous distress also under-
take and carry through the alterations and
reconstructions that are necessary to make
the whole life consonant and well rounded.
Freedom is for all who will, and servitude
is only for those who are kept too straitly
confined by the habit of their own thought:
it is the thought that binds and it is the

thought that sets free. Suggestion is but the method of the application of this thought-power, and once harnessed it can demolish the walls and barriers of limitation that hem us in, it can enable us to scale the heights of the seemingly impossible, and it can set us free to realize in the most practical manner that, even as the text ascribed to these remarks, "Man is the master of his fate."

Printed in the United Kingdom
by Lightning Source UK Ltd.
101638UKS00001B/57